Money is a Defense

Simple Enough for Everyone to Understand,

Practical Enough to Apply to All,

So Critical It Will Change Your Life

By Pastor Jim Krohn

Ground and Pillar Essentials
Southeast Bible Baptist Church
1850 Fairport-Nine Mile Point Road
Penfield, NY 14526
(585) 388-0850
www.myground.org

ISBN: 9781890120917
Library of Congress Control Number: 2013955932

Daystar Publishing
P.O. Box 464
Miamitown, Ohio 45041

To my beloved wife, Andrea. Her willing spirit and lack of covetousness made it easy for me to leave a well-paying job and go into the ministry.

OTHER BOOKS BY THIS AUTHOR

BIBLICAL YOUTH WORK: A very Biblical look at youth ministry written by someone in the trenches for twenty plus years. It breaks a lot of conventions and deals with some of the problems in youth ministries today. This book not only looks at how to run an activity, but lays out the Biblical basis and purpose of youth work, deals with important topics, and examines relationships. Not just a book for youth leaders - ***this book is for teens, parents, and pastors alike!***

FOREWARD

In February 2011, I was speaking in NY and I heard Pastor Jim Krohn speak on finances. I was so impressed by what I heard that I challenged him to put it in a book. I think this material needs to be in every home in America. This topic is of critical importance to Christians today. As a businessman, I owned 457 apartments and when someone would put in an application for one of my apartments I would always run a credit check on them. I was shocked and amazed by how many people have misused their credit cards, accumulated debt, and ruined their financial future. I know firsthand how to handle money wisely and, from my apartments, I know firsthand how many people handle it foolishly.

It should be in every home. Every teenager should read this book and have to take a test on it. They ought to have it as required reading and required study. Every Christian school should require this book as part of their curriculum. This book should be done for devotions in the home.

This is one of the most amazing books that I have ever read on finances. I highly recommend this book.

As owner of seven businesses that grossed hundreds of millions of dollars, I know the importance of the material in this book. It would revolutionize the lives not only of young people, but of adults and could be used by many to help get out of debt. If Christians would put this into practice, it would have a tremendous impact on churches. Read this book!

Dr. Russell Anderson

MONEY IS A DEFENSE

APPENDIX

"Way More Important than Most People Realize"

#1
Finances Are About More Than Money

A big mistake many people make is to think that finances are only about money. Well-meaning people make spiritual sounding statements like:

"It doesn't matter how much money you make if you love the Lord."

"Money does not buy happiness."

"Most rich people are unhappy."

"Rich people have a harder time getting saved."

"It is better to live by faith."

"Money does not make you spiritual."

"God will take care of me."

"God blesses the righteous."

Yes, it is better to live by faith. Yes, many rich people are unhappy. All of these statements are true to an extent. The problem is that people draw wrong conclusions from these true statements. These wrong conclusions then lead to errors that ***ruin people's lives*** or ***cripple them in their service*** for the Lord.

"Really?" Yes, really. Finances are way more important than people realize and are about a lot more than just money. This list will explain what I mean.

"WHY SHOULD I READ THIS BOOK?"

1. This book may save you hundreds of thousands of dollars.

No, I am not exaggerating. Hundreds of thousands of dollars are at stake. Your entire financial future could be revamped and changed in the most dramatic fashion. More than that, if you are a parent, it can have an even more dramatic impact on the life of your children.

2. This book may save you countless arguments.

Money is at the heart of many marriage arguments. I've read both secular and Christian sources that place money among the top three issues that couples fight about. Some even put it as number one. Probably every couple that has been married for a long period of time has had at least one argument about money.

Shouldn't Christians be more spiritual than that? Maybe, but I have learned that it is pointless to even think that way.

The fact is that not all Christians are spiritual and even the most spiritual Christian can have a bad day.

What about baby Christians? Do we expect them to be perfectly spiritual immediately upon salvation? It is foolish to think that people will not fight about money simply because they are Christians.

3. This book may save your marriage:

Money issues can eventually lead to unhappiness or divorce. How does a couple "fall out of love" with each other? I understand that love should be more a decision than a feeling and that this should never happen in a marriage. Still, how do couples that were madly in love with each other on the way to the marriage altar end up growing cold or even hating each other? They end up that way because they fight a lot and treat each other differently than they did before they were married.

Don't misunderstand me. I am not saying that every argument a couple has is because of finances. However, many non-financial arguments have finances contributing in an underlying fashion. Many marriage arguments are over stupid things. Sometimes the start of an argument is so trivial that couples don't even remember what they were fighting over when they get to the end. Arguments like that are caused by stress. Stress contributes to them fighting over things that would never bother them if they were in a better situation.

Nothing contributes to stress in a marriage like a bad financial situation. This environment of stress creates many opportunities to fight. All those fights lead to unhappy marriages and divorces. I wish that were not true. It shouldn't be true, but it is.

4. ***This book may save (or at least greatly help) your church:***

Churches are financially broke. If you are in a church that has plenty of money, you are the exception. Most churches can't hire the staff they would like, can't pay them what they deserve, can't run the number of buses they want, etc. God's people should give more! I've heard that preached many times. Amen, amen, amen! I agree, but is the lack of giving always because God's people are stingy? Haven't you ever met a Christian who desired to give, but just didn't have any money?

The widow who gave two mites, certainly gave more than everyone else because she gave all. However, would God have thought less of her if she had more to give and still gave it all? What if her all was two shekels instead of two mites, and she gave all of that? Yes, I know that God can multiply small amounts. I know I am at risk here and that some will accuse me of being carnal, but I would rather have the one who gave all, have more to give! The fact is that God's work requires money, and He has set some spiritual laws in motion that He does not normally override - more on that in future chapters.

God's work suffers because of a lack of money.

This is caused by the sin of God's people, but not all of the problem is because God's people are unwilling to give. Some of it is because God's people have made mistakes with their finances and cannot give what they would like.

5. This book may get the Gospel to a foreign land:

Missionaries have to drag their families all over the country for years trying to raise support. This issue is related to the above (churches being broke). The problem is probably a little more pronounced with missionaries because they are dependent on offerings above the tithe. What is happening to those people in foreign countries while a missionary has to work so hard to raise support? What is happening to them when a missionary does not make it to the field? They die in their sins.

THIS IS IMPORTANT

Finances are about more than the amount you have in the bank. What I am telling you is that the well-being of your finances affects more than just your checkbook. It impacts every area of your life. It can destroy your marriage, it can keep you from service, it can hurt your church, and it can keep the Gospel off of foreign fields.

But doesn't God take care of His own? Yes, under certain conditions. Of course, failure is not on God's part. If He does not bless us, it is not His fault, but ours. His blessings are based on our actions. God always ***desires*** to take care of His people and He is always ***able*** to take care of His people, but sometimes the decisions of His people get in the way of His blessings. Too many Christians make spiritual sounding statements and ignore what God has said in His Word about His blessings - more on that in future chapters.

Even if you are on blessing ground, how much will you be blessed? Do you want to put your spirituality to the test every day because of bad decisions you have made in the area of your finances? Wouldn't it be nice not to have financial pressures on your marriage relationship?

Wouldn't it be nice to be able to give more to the church or be able to afford to go on missions trips? Wouldn't it be better if your church members were able to give enough so that your church did not need to take out a mortgage in your next building program?

Sure, read this book if you would like to have more money in your checking account,... but that is only one small reason why you should read this book.

Finances impact EVERY area of your life.

"It's Not Persecution. It's Your Stupidity"

#2
You Reap What You Sow

In addition to the many spiritual sounding statements listed in chapter one, persecution is sometimes blamed for a person's financial difficulty. Much of this is really a cover for mistakes or outright sin. In contrast to what some would have you to believe, we bear a significant portion of the burden when it comes to our financial state. Let's take a look at what the Bible really says about finances.

> *"I have been young, and now am old; yet have I not seen the righteous forsaken, nor his seed begging bread."*
>
> Psalms 37:25

This verse tells us that it is the righteous for whom the Lord will provide. While everyone who is saved may have imputed righteousness, not all of them act righteous. Given that this verse is in Psalms, it is fair to say that this promise is to those who act righteous. This verse is, after all, a report from a man that judged this with his eyes. He saw people acting righteous and he saw that God provided for them.

"The sluggard will not plow by reason of the cold; therefore shall he beg in harvest, and have nothing."
Proverbs 20:4

In contrast to those who make it seem as if God will provide for all His children, this verse says that the sluggard will have nothing. Yes, God owns the cattle on a thousand hills, but He is under no obligation to give any of that cattle to a sluggard. That does not mean that He won't make an exception. He is a gracious God, but you have no right to count on it.

This point may be obvious to most people so I won't belabor it, but if you have any doubt I would suggest you do your own study. Investigate what God says in the Bible about sluggards and slothful people.

"For even when we were with you, this we commanded you, that if any would not work, neither should he eat."
II Thessalonians 3:10

Does this verse make it sound as if God will take care of you financially no matter how you behave? To me it sounds like the opposite. Not only is God under no obligation to take care of you, but maybe I shouldn't help you out either (if I judge you to be lazy).

This next passage is long, but is important for context. Everyone loves the last verse in it, Philippians 4:19, but they often leave out the context. I will comment on it as we look at the passage:

"But I rejoiced in the Lord greatly, that now at the last your care of me hath flourished again; wherein ye were also careful, but ye lacked opportunity."
Philippians 4:10

This was a people that took care of Paul very well. They were very giving.

> *"Not that I speak in respect of want: for I have learned, in whatsoever state I am, therewith to be content."*
>
> Philippians 4:11

I love how Paul makes it known that his need for a love offering was not because he was covetous.

> *"I know both how to be abased, and I know how to abound: every where and in all things I am instructed both to be full and to be hungry, both to abound and to suffer need."*
>
> Philippians 4:12

Paul had learned how to live on almost nothing. He lived in a time that was impoverished compared to today.

> *"I can do all things through Christ which strengtheneth me."*
>
> Philippians 4:13

> *"Notwithstanding ye have well done, that ye did communicate with my affliction."*
>
> Philippians 4:14

Paul compliments them on how they have given him love offerings and eased his sacrifice. It should be our goal to do that for others, especially our pastors.

> *"Now ye Philippians know also, that in the beginning of the gospel, when I departed from Macedonia, no*

church communicated with me as concerning giving and receiving, but ye only."

Philippians 4:15

"For even in Thessalonica ye sent once and again unto my necessity."

Philippians 4:16

This was not a one time thing. They had a hand in supporting him and helping to start a lot of churches. I would love to have that testimony in heaven.

"Not because I desire a gift: but I desire fruit that may abound to your account."

Philippians 4:17

Paul says that the best part about their giving was not that he got more, but that they had more rewards in heaven. God notices when we give.

"But I have all, and abound: I am full, having received of Epaphroditus the things which were sent from you, an odour of a sweet smell, a sacrifice acceptable, wellpleasing to God."

Philippians 4:18

"But my God shall supply all your need according to his riches in glory by Christ Jesus."

Philippians 4:19

Which brings us to the verse that people often quote when in need. After looking at the passage, isn't it foolish to twist that verse and use it to say that God will supply everyone's need? I think it is far more reasonable to say that God will meet the need of those who meet the needs of others. The context is plain. This verse was written to a group of people that was very giving and took care of God's man. If that is not you, then you really can't claim Philippians 4:19.

Now consider this very common passage.

> *"Be not deceived; God is not mocked: for whatsoever a man soweth, that shall he also reap."*
> Galatians 6:7

This verse is even more extreme. Fundamentalists usually only apply this to more commonly preached-against sins, but why wouldn't it also apply to the financial area of your life? If you make lots of bad financial decisions, or are slothful, or refuse to give, you ***are*** going to reap what you sow. The verse warns you not to be fooled - be not deceived!

Too many Christians think they can get away with mocking God.

Thinking that you won't reap what you sow is mocking God. Read that verse again - God is not mocked.

> *"For he that soweth to his flesh shall of the flesh reap corruption; but he that soweth to the Spirit shall of the Spirit reap life everlasting."*
> Galatians 6:8

> *"And let us not be weary in well doing: for in due season we shall reap, if we faint not."*
> Galatians 6:9

God promises to bless if you are faithful. To apply this in the area of finances - keep doing well and you will prosper financially over time.

> *"As we have therefore opportunity, let us do good unto all men, especially unto them who are of the household of faith."*
>
> Galatians 6:10

Our goal should be to have the ability to bless others. This even applies to our money.

This passage teaches us that we reap what we sow. If we plant radishes, we won't be harvesting corn. If you have financial issues, there is most likely a problem with what you have sown.

Too many people make spiritual-sounding statements about money to cover up their bad decisions.

The poorest of those living in America live like a king when compared to those in history. A single change of raiment used to be the equivalent of a month's pay and someone was lucky if they owned one change of clothes. How many changes of clothes does the average person have today? Think of how much food, clothes, etc. we throw away!

We live in such a prosperous time that there is ***almost no reason*** why every Christian can't be doing well financially. Think about it. God is on the Christian's side. God wants to bless. We live in the most affluent country in the world during the most affluent time in history. If you are not doing well, you are doing something wrong.

It's not God's lack of provision and it's not some terrible persecution. A lot of times God's people struggle financially because they made bad decisions.

YOU HAVE TO DO SOMETHING

"Well, I still think that God will take care of me no matter what"...That is a foolish thought that people do not apply to other areas of their lives. Do you ever go to the doctor? Why would you go to the doctor when God will take care of you? Of course God will take care of you, but he has also given us doctors. A doctor could be one of the means that God uses to take care of you. Do you jump off a cliff without a parachute and ask for a miracle on the way down? You can do that if God is taking care of you, right? Of course not, but some people are doing that financially.

God is under no obligation to help you financially if you are an idiot.

I'm not saying He won't help you. He sometimes does. More than that, if you have made financial mistakes and have repented of them, I believe God will be gracious to you. However, don't willingly put yourself in that position. Don't put yourself in the position where, because of bad decisions on your part, you have to continually go to God for a miracle.

Not everyone who is an idiot (financially) realizes it.

Most people who make financial mistakes do so because they do not realize that they are making them! I think the vast majority of Christians are hurting their financial future. The problem is not just that God will not bless your dumb financial mistakes, it is that so many Christians make those mistakes.

I am convinced that the financial problems encountered by most Christians are merely the result of them reaping what they have sown for years prior.

Even if a Christian is not completely struggling, they are probably not as blessed as they could be and they don't even realize it. Not everyone who makes financial mistakes realizes that they are making financial mistakes. In fact, most don't. There is much in American culture today that encourages these mistakes and makes them natural. Since we reap what we sow, we need to learn how to sow in the right way to be fully blessed of the Lord.

Most of our financial problems are self-inflicted.

"Money is a Defense"

#3
Something Money has in Common with Wisdom

This book takes its title from a very interesting verse in the book of Ecclesiastes.

> *"For wisdom is a defence, and money is a defence: but the excellency of knowledge is, that wisdom giveth life to them that have it."*
>
> Ecclesiastes 7:12

I would rather be wise than rich. You can lose riches, but you can't lose your wisdom. Wisdom also gives you a leg up on going to heaven - a wise person is more likely to get saved than a rich person. However, ***both*** wisdom and money have something in common - they are both a defense.

The context of Ecclesiastes is that we live in a sin-cursed world that is full of vanity. Living for yourself, accomplishments, education, and pleasure is all vanity. The only conclusion that you can draw from the book is that we should live for God (Ecc. 12:13).

However, in the midst of all the vanity, there are some bright spots in the book. Good friends (Ecc. 4:8-12) are a blessing that can lessen the vanity that we are surrounded by, or, at the very least, help us through that vanity. Likewise, wisdom (in our verse above) is an excellent defense against the vanity of this world. Would anyone argue with the concept that the wisdom of the wise spares them some of the vanity of this life? We have already covered that we are going to reap what we sow. The foolish are going to make more mistakes and do more dumb things than the wise. Our verse says that wisdom is a defense against all of that.

Wait! According to the Bible, money is just as much as a defense against the vanity and trouble of this life as wisdom is. I have a very, very unspiritual sounding saying that I like to use:

Nothing takes stress out of a situation like $10,000 sitting in your bank account.

As an example, take the Christian family that is living paycheck to paycheck with lots of personal debt. Let's say it happens that in one week the car has a major breakdown and the hot water heater quits. This type of thing happens in our sin-cursed world. Now, let's remember that we have an adversary (the devil) and add him to our scenario - remembering that he is stirring things up in the background. Maybe there is also some blame that can passed around, maybe there are other stresses at work or with the family, maybe they are just tired, or maybe there is also some sickness in the family. Is every Christian family always going to handle that situation well? How much easier would that situation be for them if, instead of the debt, they had $10,000 in the bank?

"Oh, but God will take care of..." Stop! What if they are reaping what they have sown? *"Well, if they were spiritual..."* Stop! Every family is not as spiritual as they should be and no family is spiritual 100% of the time. *"Well, God can use the stress of their financial situation to help them grow..."* Stop! Does that mean we

should try to put ourselves under as much stress as possible all the time?

The fact is undeniable that the situation is a lot less stressful when there is a large balance in the bank account as opposed to a lot of debt. Let's not forget that there is Bible on that. In our vanity-filled and sin-cursed world, money is a defense. Living for money is wrong, but being wise with money is exceedingly right.

It's time to reset our thinking about money. Too many Christians (and maybe this is just an excuse) have an outlook that it is almost unspiritual to have money. If I had that mindset, I don't think I would save and I probably would spend more. If you have the mindset that money is a defense then, when you are out shopping, you are going to be a little bit more careful with it. You'll want to protect your bank account a little bit because it protects you (not in a way that replaces God, of course).

It is ironic that Christians who are good stewards of their finances and have lots of money in the bank would be considered unspiritual, while someone who has little money in the bank because they are spending it all the time would be thought of as spiritual. No, it is more spiritual to have more money and fewer possessions.

Money is just as much a defense as wisdom.

"Gimme"

#4
It Starts with a Mindset

Because we live in America, our churches are going to have a distinctly American culture, at least when compared to churches throughout history or in other parts of the world. There is nothing necessarily wrong with that. In general the guys in my youth group are going to play more American football than youth groups in other countries. That's okay. Our church can have an American flavor because we are trying to reach Americans. Paul became all things to all people.

However, where American culture is sinful, we need to have a sub-culture in our churches that departs from American culture and is distinctly Christian. Abortion, dress, dating, music, and television are all examples of areas where American culture is wrong and harmful to Christians. The hard thing about culture is how engrained it is in us. When you go against culture, the majority of the people think you are crazy. Tell people that dating is a somewhat modern fad and it is almost like the majority of people can't compute what you are saying. They have been programmed in a different direction.

Well, America's view of money and finances should rank near the top of any list of things wrong with American culture. As you will see more and more in this book, just about everything American culture says about money is wrong.

"But fornication, and all uncleanness, or covetousness, let it not be once named among you, as becometh saints;"

Ephesians 5:3

Covetousness is a terrible thing. It is listed with fornication and it is not to be even ***named once*** among you! It is ***not becoming*** of a child of God.

"Mortify therefore your members which are upon the earth; fornication, uncleanness, inordinate affection, evil concupiscence, and covetousness, which is idolatry:"

Colossians 3:5

Again covetousness is listed with some pretty bad company and we are to ***mortify*** it, or put it to death.

"Let your conversation be without covetousness; and be content with such things as ye have: for he hath said, I will never leave thee, nor forsake thee."

Hebrews 13:5

Our conversation, our manner of life, should be ***completely free*** of covetousness. Why? Because we have God and He will always be with us. This is why another verse (Colossians 3:5) calls covetousness idolatry.

Unfortunately, covetousness is downright acceptable in our churches. When you see how the Bible describes it, how can that be? Simple. Covetousness is acceptable in American culture so it has become acceptable in our churches.

We ought to be almost embarrassed by big purchases. Covetousness is so ***terrible*** that, for our testimony's sake, if we had a Biblical view, we would be careful in telling people about our purchases. We would want to make sure that everyone understood we could afford the purchase and that it was the Lord's will. Instead, the average Christian brags about everything they buy with no concern. Why? Because they are covetous and the covetous person likes to brag about things they have.

Being in God's will with your finances starts with a mindset.

I am going to give a lot of very practical advice in the coming pages, but it will be completely worthless if you have a covetous mindset. First, you won't want to take my advice. If that is you, if you reject my counsel, you are merely condemning yourself. Those feelings should be a warning to you that you are covetous.

Next, practical advice, no matter how awesome it is, will only take you so far.

> *"Hell and destruction are never full; so the eyes of man are never satisfied."*
>
> Proverbs 27:20

Covetous America is never satisfied. Think of all the millionaires that go broke. If you take all my advice and are still covetous, you will just waste your money on other things. You won't be able to win in the long run. God's will for your finances starts with a mindset.

Here is a simple example of what I mean by a mindset. My son, Caleb, is 19 at the time of this writing. He is working "C" shift in a plastics factory to save money while he is taking courses in our Bible Institute. He owns a car and it is currently sitting in the garage, off the road. Why? Because he is working 11pm to 7am.

I'm in bed when he works so he uses my car. I don't mind and this saves him a lot of money. The covetous teen thinks differently - I don't want to have to borrow my old man's car, I want my own set of wheels, etc.

It's terrible, but most Christians actually train their children to be covetous. They start by displaying their own covetous behavior for their children to see (sometimes making excuses for it, and sometimes not). Then they train their children up in the way they should go by letting them have covetous friends, by buying their boys car magazines, and by taking their girls to the mall all the time.

I am not saying that you can't ever go shopping. However, when the highlight of a girl's week is going shopping with her mom or her friends, what kind of mindset do you think is being trained into her?

The spiritual implications of this go far beyond finances:

> *"No man can serve two masters: for either he will hate the one, and love the other; or else he will hold to the one, and despise the other. Ye cannot serve God and mammon."*
>
> Matthew 6:24

You cannot serve God and mammon. A child that has been taught to be covetous by your behavior will have a hard time serving God.

> *"Lay not up for yourselves treasures upon earth, where moth and rust doth corrupt, and where thieves break through and steal:"*
>
> Matthew 6:19

"But lay up for yourselves treasures in heaven, where neither moth nor rust doth corrupt, and where thieves do not break through nor steal:"

Matthew 6:20

"For where your treasure is, there will your heart be also."

Matthew 6:21

There will your heart be also! Train your kids to be thinking about the mall all the time and their heart will go to the world! Do you see why the Bible says that covetousness is not even to be once named among you?! Do you see why it is unbecoming of saints?!

I have higher goals for you than that. I want you to have the right mindset as well as money in the bank. There are different categories of Christians when it comes to finances.

The wicked, or perhaps ignorant, Christian buys things without regard to whether or not they can afford it.

This Christian usually has significant credit card debt and often wonders why God does not bless them more. Unfortunately, most Christians seem to live in this spot.

The carnal (yes, carnal) Christian checks to see if they can afford something before they buy it.

This Christian usually has no credit card debt and is fairly responsible. This spot seems to be the goal of most Christians. *"If I could only get to the point where my credit cards are paid off...."* While this goal is better than the first group, it is still carnal.

The spiritual Christian knows that they can afford a purchase, but earnestly seeks the will of God before buying it.

The spiritual Christian has been living an un-covetous and industrious life. Because of this, they almost always have money in the bank. Whether or not they can afford a purchase is not the issue. They know they have money in the bank. So, when a decision has to be made, they don't go to their checkbook to see if they can afford it, they go to God to see if God wants them to make the purchase.

My friend, the difference between even the second category and this last one is profound.

You have to get your head right in order to get your checkbook right.

"When $100 is Worth More than $100"

#5
Disposable Income

"It's just $50."

"$100 isn't that much."

"I can afford $40 per month."

"It's on sale for $60."

These are things that Christians say. Yet, these are dangerous statements. Why do they say them and why are they dangerous? $50 doesn't seem like much because people quite naturally compare the $50 to their annual income. A Christian that makes $40,000 a year looks at $50 and thinks, *"That's not much at all!"*

Thinking in terms of your annual income is flawed.

It's flawed because, while $40,000 (for example) seems like a lot, the vast majority of that money is not available to you. It is tied up in your mortgage, your car payment, your heat, your groceries, etc. If you seriously had $40,000 each year that was not tied up and available to you, it would be right for you to think that $50 is not much, but that is not the case. That money is not available for you to use as you please. Most people have very little "disposable income" - income that is available for you to do with as you wish.

I don't think I am going out on a limb to say that people usually have very little disposable income. Almost all of their salary is tied up in expenses. Maybe they have only about $200 of disposable income each month. That $50 per month bill, which looked so small when compared to their annual salary, suddenly chews up a good chunk of their available cash. Let me complicate that. What happens when the furnace goes or the car breaks down?

If you only have a few hundred dollars in disposable income, you had better guard that money viciously so that you are ready for life's inevitable trials. Instead of thinking that it is nothing compared to your annual salary, you have to think of that $50/month bill as an evil attacker against your financial viability.

When is $100 worth more than $100? When you think in terms of disposable income.

You must think in terms of disposable income.

Let me give you an example from my own life. Years ago I decided to bite the bullet and sell some of my childhood things on eBay. Why bite the bullet? It was not that I was attached to them, but it involves some work and hassle to sell on eBay. I sold stuff on eBay over the course of a few years and ended up clearing about $3000. Later a need came up. I looked at my checkbook and there was about $4000 in it. It dawned on me at that point that about $3000 of it had come from what I had sold. At that moment in time, having $3000 available was worth more than you can imagine - in peace of mind, in avoiding debt - what could have been a struggle became a non-issue. I praised the Lord, and went on.

This is one of the reasons why teens and jobs are sooooo dangerous. The adult sees that the teen is only making $100 each week and lets their guard down. $100 each week? I don't have $100 to spend on myself each week! The average teen with a job has waaaayyy more disposable income than most adults. Since you can't serve God and mammon, with all that disposable income, it is very easy for teens to start serving mammon. They become carnally minded.

I was raised by a banker so I was given some common sense when it comes to money. Even though I was unsaved, when I worked I came home and gave my check to my mom. She would ask me how much I needed out of the check. Since she was working at the bank, she would deposit it when she went to work. Almost every time my answer was either $10 or $20. I used about $10 in gas every week (those were the days!) and I carried a little extra. If I had used it up, I asked for $20 so that I could replenish it. All of the rest went into my college fund.

I had more sense as an unsaved teen than most Christians have today.

I was more focused on my college than most Christians are on their Savior.

While I'm in the neighborhood, never let your teens work in a fast food restaurant. The teen years are meant for growth in the Lord, not making money (Ecclesiastes 12:1). They need to get prepared. If you ignore my counsel and have them work some meaningless minimum wage job, the least you can do is keep them out of fast food. Everyone who works in those places is between 16 and 24 and they spend all of their time listening to rock music, drinking, partying, and hitting on each other.

Christians who would never send their kid to a public school seem to have no problem allowing them to work in a far worse place - the fast food restaurant.

Worse than the atmosphere, they have the power of the paycheck over that teen. They "have" to do what the boss says or they might lose their job. I say chuck that worthless, minimum wage job.

Many, many years ago I was speaking to a pastor about this and he did not believe me. Instead, he allowed his 18-year-old son to work at a fast food place. That teen went through some ups and downs, but thankfully ending up living for the Lord. One day, that pastor asked his son if he had made any mistakes raising him. His son told him, "***Just one*** - you let me work at a fast food place. He went on to say that the temptation was worse than you can imagine.

That teen made it by the skin of his teeth. How many do not?

The temptations of a job, along with the abundance of disposable income lead to carnality among teens. Keep your teens out of jobs and, when they grow up and finally get one, teach them to squirrel that money away and limit their disposable income.

Think in terms of disposable income and teach them to do the same.

If you don't have a lot of disposable income, you must viciously protect it.

"The Scourge of America"

#6
Credit Cards

I'm sure that you all knew this chapter was coming. However, while everyone knows at some level that credit cards are dangerous, few realize how dangerous they really are. Don't skip this chapter. There will be some things in it that you most likely never knew.

Credit cards are behind a lot of our bad financial decisions. I know that they might seem harmless, but Americans carry an average of eight credit cards and have thousands of dollars in credit card debt. Truly, they are the scourge of America. Here are some reasons why:

1. You will spend more if you carry a credit card:

There have been many studies about this [see Appendix]. It has been suggested that people will spend anywhere from 5% more to 25% more if they have a credit card. Certainly, if you carry cash, you can't buy something when you don't have the cash. The ability to overspend is terrible for the undisciplined person.

More than that, there is a psychological factor in play. Maybe it has something to do with the fact that you are getting something now, but not having to pay for it until much later. Maybe it just hurts less to swipe a card instead of counting out the cash. Whatever the reason, you will spend more money if you carry a credit card.

2. *You lose your grace period when you carry a balance:*

Very few realize this. Normally, with a credit card, if you buy something and pay it off, you pay no interest on that item. You have until your due date to pay it without being charged interest. However, if you carry a balance of even $1 the previous month, you lose your grace period. That means you start paying interest on purchases the moment you buy them. Even if you pay off your card that month, you can't escape the interest.

For example, if you put $1,500 on a credit card and pay off $1,300, that leaves you with a $200 balance. You do NOT pay interest on $200. You pay interest on the $200 PLUS anything else you put on your card in the coming month. If you put $1,500 more on the card the coming month, at 14.99% interest you would pay about $20 interest because of that $200 balance in one month! That is the equivalent of 10% interest on your $200 balance per month (not per year)!

I know that credit card companies don't advertise that, but that’s because they do not have your best interest at heart. None of this includes any late fees or other charges which can make it much worse.

3. *Interest rates are outrageous:*

A 14.99% interest rate (or much higher) is not uncommon on credit cards. No matter how you look at it, that is not a low rate.

Here is another example: you carry a $5,000 balance, put $1,500 a month on the card and just pay off the new amount each month (so that you still end up owing only $5,000 at the end of the year) - at 14.99% you will spend about $950 in interest and at 19.99% you will flush about $1,300 a year in interest down the drain.

Do you understand the impact that this has? You haven't paid a dime down on your debt, but you have paid

$1,000 in interest! Worse, the covetous person often loses ground in that situation by accumulating debt. It doesn't take a lot of imagination to see where this can lead.

4. Paying the minimum amount is a trap:

Paying the minimum amount is another trap. Most minimum payments are on the order of 2-3%. A $2,000 balance, 15.9%, 2.08% minimum payment will take ***265 months to pay off and cost $2,944 in interest.*** At 3% minimum payment, it would take 151 months to pay off. It is obviously much worse at a higher interest rate.

Oh, it is only that much per month? I can afford that! No you can't because you will be paying that amount forever (seemingly)!

5. Convenience checks are a trap:

Why do credit card companies send you those convenience checks? It's not because they love you. It's because you start paying interest on them immediately, even if you don't carry a balance.

That stuff you are buying because it is on sale is NOT really on sale if it contributes to a credit card balance!!!

So, what should you do about your credit cards?

First, never carry a balance – EVER. *"But I need this!"* - really? Are you sure? If so, then do without in other areas, but don't carry a balance on a credit card. You are crippling your financial future if you carry a balance.

Second, if you are undisciplined (if you have a credit card balance today you are most likely undisciplined), ***get rid of your cards***. This is a hard thing to admit, but you will be helping yourself in the long run [see Appendix for a note on the emotional aspect of this].

Third, if you have a balance today, transfer that balance to a card with a low introductory rate and then DO NOT put anything else on that card. Cut up your first card and take advantage of that low introductory rate on the new card to make it easier to pay it off.

Fourth, in case you missed this point, stop using credit cards for your purchases. You will spend less!

> *"Thou shalt not lend upon usury to thy brother; usury of money, usury of victuals, usury of any thing that is lent upon usury:"*
>
> Deuteronomy 23:19

Here is a Biblical principle for you. God knows that usury (interest) can really hurt people. That is why he forbade charging it of our brothers. God knows usury hurts you and He is warning you.

At this point, the carnal Christian is rolling his eyes. This guy is a little extreme. Am I? I don't have any credit card debt. How about you? Can you tell me how much you have paid in interest in the last year? The financial stress that you put yourself under is not worth it!

Stop hurting yourself with credit cards.

"The #1 Mistake"

#7
The Thirty-Year Mortgage

Now I'm going to meddle. Most expect the credit card diatribe, but few see this one coming. As bad as credit cards are, they are not the biggest mistake. Oh, they are a colossal problem, but there is a problem that is even bigger and most don't even realize it. It is the 30-year mortgage. It has been a staple of American life for generations, but it is one of the worst financial decisions that people make. People realize credit cards are dangerous, but a 30-year mortgage is worse!

First, let me say that most people don't get a 30-year mortgage so that they can afford ***a*** house, it is so that they can afford a bigger and better house. Banks are a real problem here. They love 30-year mortgages. Realtors love the 30-year mortgage too. It means you will buy a bigger house. Most have no idea how much more money they are paying for that house. Here are some examples to help you understand:

1. *The $120,000 house:*

   A $120,000 house at 6.5% interest will cost you the following in interest:

- $ With a 15-year mortgage you will pay ***$68,159*** interest.
- $ With a 30-year mortgage you will pay ***$153,053*** interest.

2. *The choice between a $90,000 house and a $120,000 house:*

   At 6.5% interest a $90,000 home, 15-year mortgage will have about the same monthly payments as a $120,000, 30-year mortgage. I want to make sure you don't miss that. ***The two houses have the same monthly payment, but the more expensive house comes with a 30-year mortgage.*** Actually, the $90,000 home will probably have a smaller payment when you figure in taxes & PMI - more on that later.

   So that nicer home costs only $30,000 more, right? No, no, not even close. The 15-year $90,000 home will cost $141,000 over the length of the loan. The 30-year $120,000 home will cost ***$273,000*** over the length of the loan.

The bigger home actually costs you $132,000 more (because of the interest on the 30-year mortgage)!

How much disposable income do you generate each year – money left after taxes, tithe, food bills, electric, car, etc? How many years of disposable income does $132,000 represent? Selah.

Imagine how your financial situation would change if you paid off your house after 15 years? Let me put this another way - if you bought the $90,000 home, at the end of 30 years, you would have $132,000 more in your bank account than if you bought the more expensive one (actually, more if you invest that $132,000 along the way).

Then to make it worse, the average person who refinances actually lengthens the loan! Yes, that's right, it is not uncommon for a family to refinance their loan several years in and they get another 30-year loan, ensuring that they will bleed even more interest.

The taxes on the more costly home are always higher, adding to the disparity. This brings us to PMI - private mortgage insurance. It is something you have to pay until you have 20% of the value of the home paid off. PMI can easily be $60/month. It takes about 14 years to get to 20% of a 30-year mortgage. That's over $10,000 in PMI!

By the way, PMI rarely comes off automatically. If you are paying it and think you are near 20% in equity, you need to check with the bank and go through the steps to get it removed.

If you go in with a 20% down payment (so you never pay PMI) and then get a 15-year mortgage, your house will be so much cheaper!

Oh, but you just ***needed*** the bigger home. You had to have four bedrooms instead of three because you did not want your kids to have to share rooms. The more expensive house is just ***so*** much nicer. Your wife would not be satisfied with less. The nicer home is in a cul-de-sac and not a busy road so it will be so much safer. This home has a nice deck and pool. ***NO!*** You didn't just ***have*** to have it; you were covetous.

You will cripple your financial future because of your covetousness!

At this point, you are probably growing to hate me, so I should probably throw in another verse on covetousness to remind you that I am on God's side.

> *"But now I have written unto you not to keep company, if any man that is called a brother be a fornicator, or covetous, or an idolater, or a railer, or a drunkard, or an extortioner; with such an one no not to eat."*
>
> I Corinthians 5:11

You are not even supposed to keep ***company*** with a ***brother*** who is a covetous person, just like you are not even supposed to keep company with fornicators. God puts covetousness in with some pretty bad company. It is so bad that we are warned away from covetous people! It is catchy. You certainly shouldn't marry a covetous person! Compared to God, I am easy on covetousness.

What about tax deductions and mortgage interest? This falls into the category of things I shouldn't have to say out loud. Yes, paying mortgage interest is a tax deduction, but it will cost you much more. $7000 in interest is a tax deduction, but I would rather have the $7000. Believe it or not, I have had intelligent people tell me that they do not want to pay off their mortgage because they do not want to lose the tax deduction! Are you kidding me? That $7000 deduction ****may**** [see Appendix for explanatory note] save you $1000 on your taxes, but not spending the $7000 on interest saves you $7000. Hello!? This has to be either ignorance or covetousness coming up with an excuse.

There is an old saying that everyone should take to heart:

"Those that don't understand interest PAY it... those that do understand interest EARN it."

There are also other advantages to having a smaller house - less taxes to pay, less upkeep, less furniture to buy, less house to clean.

Let's think about the impact of all this. Earlier in the book, I made the controversial statement that many of our financial problems are self-inflicted. Let's imagine a couple of hypothetical situations. We will look at two couples. On the one hand we will have a couple that has applied only what we have covered so far in this book. We'll call them the Stewards. On the other hand, we will have a couple that has not. We'll call them the Smiths because they represent the average family in America.

1. Example 1: The tragedy.

Sixteen years after buying their house, both couples face a tragedy. Because of downsizing or a bad economy, the husbands both lose their jobs.

The Smiths still have 14 years left on their mortgage. Believe it or not, despite paying faithfully for 16 years, they have only paid off 24% of their mortgage. They still owe 76% of the value of their home! They also have significant credit card debt. What are they going to do? Will they lose their home? The couple tearfully asks for prayer at church and the entire church prays and feels bad for them, as they should. It is heart wrenching and it impacts every area of their life - their kid's college, everything - what are they going to do?! Why hasn't God provided for them?

The Stewards finished paying off their mortgage a year ago. Since they never carried any credit card debt, they have been able to save a little money all along. Oh, they haven't lived as richly as the Smiths, but they have had a good life that was free of financial stress. On top of that, they saved all of the money that would have gone to their mortgage the last year. They were considering using it on their dream trip, but God had not given them peace about using it, even though it was in the bank. Now they know why. They give thanks and praise to God at church for how He has provided for them and they also ask for prayer for God's will on the next job.

Tell me that this couldn't happen in your church or in your life. We live in the days of downsizing. Rare it is that someone works 35 years for the same company and retires.

Why is it that God took care of the Stewards and not the Smiths? The fact is that God took care of both and one couple was covetous (and stupid). Now, God may bail the Smiths out - for His name's sake, because He loves His people - but He is not obligated to and He likely won't do it in style. Read those verses again about what God thinks about covetousness. Do you want to bank on God rescuing you from your sinful decisions?

2. Example 2: The need.

In this example, it has again been 16 years since they purchased their homes. This time, they both keep their jobs. However, during a church service God impresses on their hearts the importance of a great need. Maybe the need is a building program, or a missionary work. Maybe God leads them to take a mission trip to Africa and the cost will be thousands of dollars. For the sake of this example, it doesn't really matter what the need is, just that there is a spiritual need that God lays on their heart.

The Stewards, the couple with their house paid off, get excited when this happens. They talk it over, they pray it over, and the leading is unmistakable. God wants them to meet that need and they give. They give liberally and God blesses them even more. They hear reports of how God used their finances and it warms their hearts. Their kids see this and the faith of their teenage kids grows. They have a story and a testimony that they give for the rest of their lives. They end up blessed here on earth, they have rewards in heaven, and the heart of their family is drawn toward heavenly things *(...for where your treasure is, there will your heart be also...).*

The Smiths - do we even need to talk about them? They have been under financial stress for years. Financial subjects wear them out. Maybe one of them is stirred spiritually while the other is not and they fight about what to do. Maybe they get bitter about how the preacher/God is always after money. Their kids see all this and they wonder where the reality of Christianity is. Whatever happens, they certainly don't give like God would have wanted them to. Maybe God doesn't even bother to touch their heart in the service because He knows that they have not put themselves in a position to be used. *"Why doesn't God ever speak to me?!"* It might be because of the decisions you have made. That thought ought to frighten you.

One couple misses the will of God!

Mistakes that the Smiths made years ago have hamstrung them. They don't get to experience the joy or the blessing or the fruit that God wanted them to experience.

Multiply this story by the majority of the church and I think you will see why God's work often struggles financially. Some people want to give, but just don't have the means because of their mistakes.

We live in the most affluent country in the world during the most affluent time in history. We have God who wants to bless us. Yet, God's work often struggles financially.

It is because of our sin and bad decisions!

Do you think I am exaggerating? For the first time I will drop Russell Anderson's name. Most know him to be a multi-millionaire. Hyles-Anderson college is named after him. He has given more money to the cause of Christ than perhaps anyone else. When I presented this material in a Sunday School class that he attended, he about came unglued. He said that this is what is wrong (monetarily) in Christianity and that everyone needs to hear it. It was at this point that he said that he would ask God to whip me if I did not write this book. You might be able to dismiss my counsel, but I am confident that he knows more about finances than you do.

What should you do? What am I telling you to do in terms of buying a house?

$ Live in an apartment a year longer.
$ Live super-frugally in order to save money.
$ Buy a smaller house.
$ Refinance down to 15 years or pay ahead on your 30-year mortgage.

Do whatever it takes to get a 15-year mortgage.

"The Mistake with the Best Excuses"

#8
Cars

I view cars as necessary evil - and you should too. You should never view them as a toy or a luxury item that you desire. Unfortunately, this is the mistake that has the best excuses. Credit cards I can tell you to avoid, I can condemn 30-year mortgages, but only in extreme cases can I tell you to live without a car.

First, let me give you my testimony. At the time of this writing, it is 2011. Since about 1992, I have mostly had two cars in our family and, during these past 19 years, I have never bought a car.

I said, I have never bought a car -
not just a new car, I have not bought any car.

How can that be? Well, I have been blessed. I have gotten some from relatives and I have gotten some from church members. Once I had a guy show up in our church, he stayed for a couple of weeks, he gave me a car, and then disappeared. No, he was not an angel unawares, because he smoked. I figure God's angels don't smoke - the devil's angels do. :-)

I literally could tell you story after story of how God provided for me. Oh, I did not always drive nice cars. Also, in the interest of full disclosure, there were times when I only had one car on the road. For a time, while I would be picking up teens for church, a girl that used to be in my youth group (and used to get picked up by us), would get my family for church. An imposition? Actually, she loved it. She got to pick ***us*** up!

I should also give you some context by telling you that I did not go full time in the ministry until 2002. Until that time, I had a great, well paying job. I just chose to drive older cars. This allowed me to give a lot more to missions and other needs.

So, how did this happen? First off, I prayed about it and God answers prayer. Secondly, I was...

> *"Let your conversation be without covetousness; and be* ***content with such things as ye have****: for he hath said, I will never leave thee, nor forsake thee."*
> Hebrews 13:5

I had it within my power to buy a car, even a new car. I just had to adjust my missions giving and I could have a new car, but that might have resulted in missionaries coming off the field. *"Don't you feel deprived?"* Are you kidding me? Do you know how cool it is to watch God provide for you? You can keep your new cars; God's provision is better.

Thirdly, I could live on hand-me-down cars because God's people generally get rid of cars while they still have a lot of life in them. I don't want to take God out of the equation, but I drive my cars into the ground and most people don't.

You might not be able to duplicate what I have done - although I encourage you to pray about it if you feel led - but you can drive much cheaper cars. Here are some of the good excuses that people use to buy new cars:

1. *I want to save money on repairs:*

I have driven some of the junkiest junk on the planet and yet I spend only about $75/month/car on repairs - often less. Compare that to a $350/month new car payment. I think I am coming out ahead to the tune of thousands of dollars each year per car. This doesn't even consider the fact that newer cars are not maintenance-free. You are still going to have to replace brakes and things on them eventually.

You would think, looking at that math, that people would never buy new cars, but the opposite is true. Instead, I hear things like, “A $500 car repair bill? I’m sick of these repairs, I’m getting a brand-new car.” Sure, but the last time you put money in the car was six months ago.

You would have to have a $500 car repair bill two months out of three to approach the payments of a new car.

Think about it. How come no one ever says, "I'm sick of these new car payments?" If you do your own repairs (I don't), it gets even better. In fact, it gets much better.

Driving an older car also ***saves you a lot of money on insurance.*** Since all my cars are ten years old, I never carry collision on them.

2. *I need something reliable so that I don't break down:*

Again, I’ve driven a lot of junk and have rarely broken down – and I beat my cars to death! Don’t newer cars break down too? Unless you’re driving in dangerous neighborhoods or in the middle of nowhere, breaking down is no big deal, especially in the days of cell phones.

Yes, it is a hassle. Yes, it is inconvenient to break down, but compare that to the cost. Perhaps you break down once in ten years and it costs you an hour of hassle. Yet, driving that old car saves you $3300 each year - that works out to be $33,000 over ten years. How much do you make per hour that money like that is not worth a breakdown or two?

Let's face it, though these may be good excuses on the surface, they are still just excuses. The real reason for buying a new car is that people want to drive something new and nice. It's covetousness. Maybe there is also a touch of pride - I deserve a nice car, I shouldn't have to put up with the hassle of breaking down, etc. This is an expensive sin you are committing. You do realize that a new car loses 20% of its value the first year, right?

Don't even get me started on leasing. It saves a little money on the payment each month, but then you have to give the car back when the lease is over! *"I could buy this car, but at the same monthly payment I could lease this nicer car. It is the car of my dreams. What a deal!"* No. It's covetousness again. There is a reason why dealers WANT to lease you cars – they make out like bandits. They are not leasing you a car, they are "fleecing" you a car. Don't be taken in by smooth-talking salesman and too-good-to-be-true deals.

Russell Anderson, the multi-millionaire, told me that he won't buy a car unless it has 20,000 miles on it. He said that a car loses its value the fastest in the first 20,000 miles. As an added bonus, after 20,000 miles all of the initial factory problems have been worked out of it. Now, Mr. Anderson swims in a different pond than I do. He doesn't drive the junk that I do. One of his cars is a Jaguar. The point is, he never buys a car new. Whatever your strata, whether you drive economy or luxury, it is rarely a good decision to buy new.

With teens, the decision is even more important and the contrast is even more stark. Why is a teen driving a new car? Even if it is not new, a teen will often tie up so much in an expensive car that they will save almost no money (more on this later - this ties into a critical point a few chapters from now). If I can get by driving a 10-year-old vehicle, why can't a teen? Why can't he be looking on Craig's list? If a teen just has to have a nice ride, I am concerned about that teen. To me it indicates covetousness combined with a pinch of pride and a good helping of stupidity. Everyone fawns all over him and thinks he is cool because of his nice car. No! That is from the world. Read those verses on covetousness again. People ought to look down on him and that teen ought to feel ashamed.

At this point, I am due for a disclaimer. God might give you a new car or there might be a situation where it makes sense to go new. For instance, because he knew the dealer and because of a unique situation at the dealership, my pastor was able to get a brand new mid-size sedan for about $9000. He was given 0% financing so his payments worked out to be $150/month for five years. That is a deal and a half. This is a car that normally goes for over $20,000. I would have taken that deal in a heartbeat.

Another friend of mine attacked this problem of cars in a different way. He needed two cars, but decided that he did not want to have more than one car payment. He bought one new car - it was a fairly decent deal. He paid it off over five years and then bought another one, all the while keeping the first one. If he kept each car for at least 10 years he would never have more than one payment at a time. Since they were economy cars, the payment was relatively low. If he managed to keep them for longer, he would be even farther ahead.

If you told me that you had prayed about it and that you felt God had led you down that path, I could live with that. It is not nearly as good as my way but, if God leads you that way, it is at least workable.

Here is what kills you - cycling new cars every 5-7 years, leasing, and buying luxury cars when you are not making six figures.

So, what should you do?

- $ Pray and ask for God to give you a car or to lead you to the car He wants you to have.
- $ Buy a cheaper car. Russell Anderson can drive a Jaguar. You can't. Unless you are rich, you would be far better off with an economy car.
- $ If you are buying an older car, or one that you plan on holding onto until it is very old, then buy American. The replacement parts on American cars are usually much cheaper, which saves on repairs.
- $ If you have a new car, drive it into the ground. Hold it forever and get as much value out of it as you can.
- $ Find a good mechanic - one that you can trust - or take up auto-mechanics as a hobby. If I had more time I would do it. It will save you a lot of money and it is not that difficult.

You can save A LOT of money if you drive junk.

"They Add Up"

#9
The Little Things

Little things aren't so little when you think in terms of:

DISPOSABLE INCOME!

$500/year or $1000/year is only a fraction of your total income, but it probably represents a large amount of your disposable income. Some households actually have no disposable income. In light of that, let's consider some of the following:

$ Cell Phone
$ Cable
$ High Speed Internet
$ Eating out
$ Buying your lunch instead of bringing it
$ Bottled water
$ Other convenience items
$ Clothes you don't need - I said need, not want - when your closet is full to overflowing, you don't need it
$ Refusing to shop at thrift stores and garage sales
$ Style & fashion – you have to have the name brand
$ Starbucks

Setting aside any moral elements (having cable is not a good idea because of the sin it brings into your home), every one of the items on the above list is a luxury. I am not saying that you can ***never*** have any of these things. I am saying that they are luxuries and you have to start thinking of them as such. I'm saying that it adds up and you had better realize that. You have to think in terms of disposable income.

For example, let's consider an average home that saves less than $1000 per year. Say they drop their $60/month cable bill. That $60/month doesn't seem like much compared to their $40,000/year salary, but dropping it ***doubles*** their disposable income. Say the dad buys lunch every day and spends on average $6 doing so. Over 280 working days, that's $1,680 per year!

Cell phones? The common attitude is, *"Everyone in my family absolutely needs to have one, I need to have the data plan, unlimited texting, etc."* Really? No one had cell phones 15 years ago. How did they ever survive? I know cell phones can be useful. I'm a pastor, so I carry one, but there is something wrong when more is spent on cell phones than given to missions. If you added up all the money spent by a congregation on all of their cell phones, it is probably more than that church gives to missions in a year. That can't be God's will.

Most people have so much money tied up in "little things" that it is ridiculous. No wonder you can't give to missions or the building fund. No wonder you fight with your spouse all the time. You are putting yourself under financial stress and are unable to give to important things because you have your money tied up in luxuries.

This is best illustrated by a story that was related to me by a friend who is a businessman. He was on the deacon board of a church with another man who was starting a business. My friend sold this man building material. The man starting the business asked for a line of credit from his brother in Christ and promised to pay on a certain day each month. All was well for awhile until the man started paying his bill late, or not at all. What had happened? Well, he decided to get himself a brand new truck. He also decided that, even though he only had a couple of people working for him, he needed a nice new office (luxuries). When my friend confronted him about the missed payments, the man (remember, they were both deacons on the same board) responded something like this, *"Oh, brother, I'm having a tough time right now, but I will pay you as soon as I can."* My friend responded,

"No, you are robbing me so that you can have a nice truck and a nice office."

You say, *"That's harsh."* No! My friend was right to say it because that's exactly what was happening. Why should my friend not get paid so that someone else can have a luxury? Covetousness is so engrained in us that most people are tempted to feel sorry for the one not making the payments. No, he was stealing from a brother!

Unfortunately, this happens in churches all the time. A family goes to the pastor because they are having a hard time paying their Christian school bill. *"Can we have a scholarship? Can you take an offering for us?"* Meanwhile they are driving a new car and have everything on the list from the start of this chapter. How characterless! ***How sinful! That's right, I said sinful. It's sin as black and dark as you can imagine.*** The Christian school struggles to get by and pays its teachers almost nothing so that you can have cable. Wicked!

Stop stealing from God so you can have high speed internet.

Whenever I am tempted to feel sorry for a family like that, I check myself by looking at a family that is actually living the Christian life. In contrast to the family who doesn't pay their school bill, you can almost always find a real Christian family. They might not make as much as the first family, they probably don't drive as nice a vehicle or have as nice stuff, but they always have their school bill paid.

This is going to sound controversial, but I mean it. I am all for charity. I want to help people, but if you want a handout from me, then I want to look at your finances. I like to give and God blesses me for it, but why should I give you my money so that you can purchase luxuries which I don't have? I would rather give my money to someone truly in need.

These little luxuries can cause us to sin in such big ways. If they cause you to not pay your school bill, or not give to missions, or - and this is the height of financial stupidity - not to tithe, then those little luxuries do a lot of damage. Way more damaging then chewing up your disposable income, they bring us under the condemnation of the Lord. We reap what we sow and if we start sowing seeds like those, we are going to reap some terrible fruit.

Other Things You Can Do

So far we have discussed little things which can be a drain on finances. In addition to looking for luxuries that you can do without, there are other little things you can do in order to save money.

The first and most obvious is to get a competitive quote. If you have to buy, then shop around, look online, etc. It amazes me how often someone just goes with the first price he gets. How lazy are you?

Another little thing you can do is negotiate. I love negotiating. If I am going to make a major purchase, after I have checked around and found the best price, I am going to try to negotiate that price down a little. I almost always get a discount above what I already found to be the best price. This applies to everything from car purchases to garage sales and everything in between.

Paying ahead is another great way to get a discount. *"Well, I can't afford to pay ahead."* If you follow the advice in this book, you will. For me, just about any major purchase starts with shopping around, is followed by negotiating down what was already the best price, and then I try to get one last discount by paying ahead.

For example, my son needed to get braces. I got some recommendations and called around. The one that I liked also ended up being the cheapest. In discussions with him, it turned out that my son really only needed braces on the uppers. He had a tooth that needed to get pulled down. If it didn't it would take out the roots of some of his other teeth (it was going sideways). The orthodontist talked about how important it was to have braces on both the upper and lower. Of course he did - he is an orthodontist. However, when I pinned him down, there was no specific reason why, it was just his preference (many orthodontists believe everyone needs braces). We went with braces only on the uppers and I negotiated a new price for that. Once I had that price, he brought out his payment plan. This led me to asking what he could do for me if I paid ahead and that question ended up saving me 10%. When it was all said and done, my son ended up with great teeth and it only cost me $2,200. I had no insurance - that was the total cost.

Another example would be my garbage pick up. The company I was with raised its rates. I went through the process and found a cheaper one. Then I called them and told them I was with a different company. Would they give me an even better rate if I switched? Yes. How about if I pay for the whole year in advance? We'll give you a month free. I ended up saving a total of about $150/year.

I go through these three steps - shop around, negotiate, pay ahead - on almost everything and I usually hit savings on at least two of the three steps, if not all three. "Well, it's too much hassle. I can't be bothered." Fifteen minutes spent on the internet and the phone saves you hundreds of dollars and you can't be bothered? How much do you make per hour? Even if the savings was only twenty or thirty dollars it would be worth way more than your normal hourly wage.

This chapter ties into a lot that we have covered already. Don't be ***covetous*** - you don't need those little things. You have to think how much impact that money makes in terms of your ***disposable income***. How you deal with money is a ***mindset***.

The little things aren't so little!

"This Doesn't Make You Smart - It Proves You're Dumb"

#10
College Done Wrong

Have you ever played with a child's "see and say" toy? The toy is a big circle with pictures around the outside and a pointer in the center. You turn the pointer towards an animal and pull the string. If it was pointing at the picture of a cow, when you pulled the string the toy would say, *"The cow says moo."* Well, if we could get a picture of a college student on that toy, when we pulled the string the toy would say, *"The liberal arts major says, 'Would you like fries with that order?' "*

Another disclaimer is needed at this point. I am for higher education. I do ***NOT*** think that all Christians should own a farm or a lawn care business. Christians ought to be lawyers and doctors. For example, several from my youth group have grown up, become pharmacists, and are serving in our church. I am not against college. As further proof of that, I want you to know that I have the following post-high school degrees:

$ Bachelors in Electrical Engineering from Rensselaer Polytechnic Institute (Cum Laude)
$ Masters in Manufacturing and Engineering Management from Clarkson University (4.0 GPA)

$ Bachelors in Pastoral Theology from Commonground Baptist Institute
$ Masters in Pastoral Theology from Commonground Baptist Institute

I give you this list, not to brag on myself, but to establish my credentials. I want to remove all doubt at the start of this chapter. I am 100% for college done right. However, I am going to be brutal toward college done wrong. Don't mistake this chapter to mean that I am against college.

WHAT IS COLLEGE DONE WRONG?

College done wrong is college without purpose. It is going to college for the sake of going to college. It is going to college because you don't know what else to do. It is being in your second year of college and not knowing what your major is yet. What are you thinking?

It is now time for another installment of "Things I Shouldn't Have to Say Out Loud." (TM)

The only reason to go to college is to make more money when you graduate.

College is an earnings investment. You ought to make more because of your diploma. Otherwise you are wasting your time. Worse, you are wasting thousands of dollars. College is not cheap. Any kid going to college should have a plan and be able to see how this time in college will cause him to make more money than if he didn't go. If not, he is setting back his financial future for years.

Some people might object - *"Isn't learning for the sake of learning, a good thing?"* Sure, but in the real world you have to pay bills. If you want to learn, read a book. You don't have to spend tens of thousands of dollars to learn.

Unless you are independently wealthy, college for the sake of college merely incurs debt!

It's actually worse than the college debt by itself. A teen that starts to work right out of high school can earn a good amount of money during the time that another teen is in college. One teen is earning money. The other is incurring debt. Again, I am not against college, but you better have a plan. You ought to know, before going to college, how attending college will lead you to a specific kind of job that will more than pay for your time in college.

For example, I have already mentioned some teens in my youth group that became pharmacists. They incurred tremendous debt, but that debt led them to a job that gave them a tremendous salary.

Another teen in my youth group managed to get into a radiology technician program at the local community college. It was a little extra work to get into that program, but now a job with a good starting salary awaits graduation. Since the program was at a community college, it was much cheaper than most college degrees.

One of my daughters did a phlebotomy vocational program that cost $2,000. She was done with her course and her internship in about two months total. Shortly after that she was hired full-time by one of the local hospitals. She asked to be put in their outpatient labs so that they would never even ask her to work on Sunday. At 18 years old she had a decent paying job (in a good environment), with vacation time, personal days, free tuition if she wanted to continue her medical education, and a retirement account. She now is working days while she lives at home and is taking night school classes from our Bible Institute so that she can be a Christian School teacher down the road. It has turned out to be a great plan! When I was an unsaved student at a high profile engineering college, I looked down on people who went to a vocational school instead of college. That was stupid of me.

Others from my youth group are studying engineering, nursing, etc. The specific field is not what I care about. The point is that you need a plan whereby college leads to being well compensated for your time there.

The exception to all this might be Bible college. Obviously, you don't go to Bible college to get rich. There are ministry reasons to go to college. Perhaps a teen is struggling spiritually and one year in a Bible college is a spiritual investment. I don't have a problem with that. I am all for spending money for a spiritual investment.

Some Spiritual Thoughts

Although not related directly to finances, I can't talk about college without mentioning some important spiritual considerations.

Secular college needs to be treated with the utmost caution.

College is an extremely wicked place. All those young, unsaved people together with no supervision - that's a recipe for sin. I would never recommend that a person go away to a secular college. Living in the dorms would be like living in a cesspool. Many teens have not made it for the Lord because of college dorms. I know of one who survived it. He told me that during his two years in the dorms he took the worst spiritual beating of his life. His words, not mine. Most teens and parents have no idea.

If you have a local college, if they can live with their parents, if they can keep going to their church, if they have a good support group, then maybe. I'm smelling a lot of "if" coming off that plan, but it is possible. I won't put God in a box, but this is something that needs to be entered into with the utmost prayer.

Christian college needs to be approached with the utmost caution.

The answer is not necessarily Christian college. If everyone at Christian college lived like the Apostle Paul, it would be a great environment. I would encourage everyone to go. Unfortunately, that is not the case. There are a lot of wicked kids at Christian college. There are a lot of kids that are sent to Christian college by parents hoping that they will grow spiritually. There are a lot of bad kids that get kicked out and I am sure that they take some good kids with them.

One of the most dangerous times in the life of a second generation Christian is when they graduate from high school. So much changes after graduation and those changes are all opportunities for our spiritual enemy to get into a Christian's life. A Christian college is a much less sinful environment than a secular college, but in some ways it can be just as dangerous. Kids often let their guard down in a Christian environment. Plus, the "I'm a

Christian it's okay to do this" is working against you. Don't take Christian college lightly.

Certainly, going away to a Christian college is infinitely better than going away to a secular college. However, if the choice is going away to a Christian college or living at home and attending a local secular college, that's a closer call. The danger in both of those situations might be about the same.

SOME FINAL THOUGHTS

The influence of culture can be so strong. *"Today in America, a teen just has to go to college."* No, they don't. Some people really do send their kids to college thinking it makes them look smart. If there is no job at the end of that rainbow it's really just proving they're stupid.

Make college pay.

"When Freedom is Bondage"

#11
Moving Out too Soon

A teenager moving out too soon can be a horrible financial mistake. I said horrible. Yet it happens more often than not. Why?

Sometimes it is because teenagers want their freedom. They want to be on their own, they are tired of their parent's rules, or perhaps it just seems like the thing to do.

Sometimes it is because they have become romantically involved and a young man wants to move out so that he can start his own family. That is a tragedy - not that a young man wants to have a family, but that our American culture thrusts dating on pre-teenagers. The culture is so oppressively romantic that sin abounds in the teen ranks. Moving out too soon is another sin that has grown out of that culture.

Sometimes it is because they don't like their home. Often this is caused by a bad home, or Christian parents who aren't sold out for the Lord. That is another tragedy. A Christian home ought to be a refuge, a sanctuary.

Whatever the reason a teenager moves out, freedom will not be the result. Freedom - freedom to get married, freedom from a bad home - whatever freedom they seek will likely result in financial bondage.

Moving out costs thousands upon thousands of dollars. It's not just the rent, it's the electric and the phone and the heat, etc. A teen can be saving THOUSANDS of dollars at home instead of wasting it on their own place. Do you want to give your kids a financial head start in life? Let them live with you.

I tell my kids often that they can live with me forever.

I love my kids. They are a joy to have around. My best nights are ones that I can spend with my family. It will be a sad day when they move out. I realize it will happen one day. In most cases it has to happen, but they can stay with me for as long as they need. Think how easy it is for a teen working full-time to save $15,000 to $20,000 a year if they are living at home. My son's goal is to have $100,000 in the bank before he moves out. He might not attain that goal, but I am glad he has it.

"Aren't you worried about them being lazy and sponging off of you?"

The scope of this book is too narrow to encompass all of your bad parenting.

Seriously? Sponges? If you raised a sponge, you have already failed in many ways as a parent. If you have allowed your kids to develop laziness as a character trait, if you have raised kids who are covetous and spend all their money (or yours), if you have raised kids who won't get a job and want to spend all of their time playing video games, then, yes, kick them out. At that point it is best to push them out the door. You can hope that the pressures of the real world, the bills they will have to pay, and the hard times they will have to face will accomplish what you failed to do as a parent.

I know covetousness and laziness are acceptable sins in our society, but they shouldn't be. If you find yourself in the position where you have to kick them out because they are lazy, you are not much different than the parent that has to send their kid to a boy's home. In both situations there is a terrible character flaw that needs to be corrected and the parent doesn't feel that they can do it. It is much better to raise your kids to have a work ethic and not be materialistic so that you don't have to kick them out prematurely.

> *"A good man leaveth an inheritance to his children's children: and the wealth of the sinner is laid up for the just."*
>
> Proverbs 13:22

This should be our goal, or at least part of our goal as parents. We want to rear kids who love the Lord, but we also want to rear kids that can be all they can for the Lord. Our finances are part of that. If you think about it, this really isn't so far off from our culture. People send their kids off to college trying to do the best for them. I want to do the best for my kids too. I want the same thing, but I have learned that what the world teaches is not the way to reach that goal. It is not necessarily best for them to go to college. In the same vein, it is not necessarily best for them to move out early.

"Do you charge your 19-year-old son rent?" No! Why would I do that? *"Because you want to teach him character."* Ugh, no, I taught him that when he was two years old and I have reinforced it ever since. You're thinking wrong. He has character. At this point I am trying to give him a financial future. I have no problem with a parent charging rent if there is a need, but most parents charge rent because they are covetous (they want money) or because they want to encourage their kids to move out.

You have to change your way of thinking. If my goal is to help give them a financial future, then charging rent works against that. In my world, my son (who is not perfect - don't misunderstand me) is staying at home and saving money for a house. If I charge him rent, I am not encouraging him to move out, I would be delaying him moving out. I would be slowing down his savings.

In modern America, it seems to be the goal of parents to have their kids move out. That is not the goal! Cultivate a family life where you enjoy your kids, they are submissive and helpful, and they ***want*** to stay. Rear your kids so that they can be all God wants them to be, including being financially well-prepared.

Moving out too early brings financial bondage.

"How the Average Teen Sets Back His Financial Future by 20 Years"

#12
How This All Ties Together

Just as a small change at the helm can greatly alter the destination of a ship over a great distance, so a small change in the financial planning of a teen can greatly impact his lifetime financial destination. I want to help everyone reading this book, but I especially want to help teens. American culture is not your friend. It seems as if everything in American culture is designed to hurt your financial future.

If you are not a teenager, maybe one day you will have teenagers. If not that, maybe you can influence teens. The advice in this chapter might be too late for some of you, but it is critical and it is definitely counter-culture. It is also common sense and it needs to be said.

I've warned about many financial mistakes in this book. Most teens, without counsel, will probably make most of them. Let's talk about the average teen mistakes:

Most are raised to be covetous. Most get a job too early. Instead of helping their financial future, in an ironic fashion, it usually hurts it. They have too much disposable income and this, at a young age, confirms their covetousness and sets them to following mammon. This becomes a habit they take with them all their lives (hurting their financial future).

Teens almost always spend too much on a car. Perhaps this is even an extension of their covetous upbringing - they've been looking at car magazines all their lives. Either way, the car and insurance use up all the money that their covetousness doesn't claim - almost ensuring that they carry very little savings out of the teen years.

Then they move out too soon. Maybe it is because it is the final extension of their freedom - they've had a car and a job for so long that it seems like the next step. Maybe it is because they can't get along with their parents. Maybe it is because they are romantically involved. Whatever the reason, they miss the best opportunity to save money that they will have in their entire life.

On top of that, it is possible that they have incurred debt that is difficult to repay because they did college wrong. College is good, but only if it leads to a job that can pay off that debt. Even if they did college okay, they certainly weren't saving money in all those years at college.

THE END RESULT

The end result of all these bad decisions is that, at the very least, it greatly impacts their house purchase.

The teen that MAKES these mistakes is far more likely to have no savings and/or lots of debt. He is far more likely to delay a house purchase. Perhaps he doesn't buy one until his late twenties. He is also far more likely, because of less savings, to go with a thirty-year mortgage.

The teen that AVOIDS these mistakes is far more likely to have a sizable savings and a good house down payment. He is far more likely to purchase a home earlier - perhaps in his early to mid-twenties. He is also far more likely to get a fifteen-year mortgage.

One teen makes decisions that means he buys a house at 28 and has it paid off when he's 58.

Another teen makes decisions that allows him to buy a house at 24 and have it paid off at 39!!!

Do you understand the difference this can make in a person's life? Many a parent would say that they want to give their child a good education. Well, start by giving them a good financial education. It is far more important. Which teen are you? Which teen are you raising?

Some might accuse me of exaggerating. Actually, I'm doing the opposite. I'm under-selling the idea. For the teen that lives this book, having their house paid off at 39 is almost a worst case scenario. My son is actually living an extreme version of this advice. I hesitate to use him as an example because he is only 19. In fact, I ask you to pray for him as you read about him because using him makes his life and his financial life a target of our enemy.

He is called of God to the ministry. In a very practical way, he realizes that assistant pastors do not make a lot of coin. He has seen how working a full-time, secular job can hamstring an assistant pastor. So, while he is taking courses in our Bible Institute, he is working a full time job, living at home, and saving money. He is taking only four courses per semester because he does not want to slow down his service in the church and because he wants to work at least 40 hours per week. This will delay his graduation slightly but, since he is living at home, he doesn't have to pay room and board so it doesn't cost him any extra to delay it. He is not in a hurry to graduate. It is not like he is going to take a church at 22 years old. Actually, he is not delayed that much because, with an eye on this plan, he took some college courses while still in high school. He is not romantically involved and does not plan to be until he nears the end of college.

He is only 19 but, if his plan works, he will graduate, be able to buy a house, pay cash for it, get married and support a family by 23 or 24. He is not doing this to get rich. It goes back to him being called. Assistant pastors don't make a lot, but that won't matter as much if he already owns his own home. Can you imagine how much easier it will be for a church to hire him?

His extreme version is not limited to the ministry. Anyone can live it. I was not exaggerating when I said that a teen who lives according to this book can have their home paid off at 39, I was under-selling it.

A teen that lives this book to the extreme can own their home by 25, easily!!!!!!

Adult, think about that. How different would your life be, how much more financial freedom would you have had if you had your house paid off by 25? ***I said 25!*** Imagine if this was the culture of America and almost everyone in the church had their home paid off by then. How much more effective could the church be for Christ? Think of the impact on building funds, missions giving, bus routes, and hiring pastors. Wow. ***Wow!***

The advice I am giving in this book can not only help your life, it can revolutionize the cause of Christ.

Again, this is not an exaggeration. If American Christianity started living this book, in less than a generation everything would be different. Everything would be better.

Don't dismiss this! Don't get pseudo-spiritual on me and tell me that God will provide. Reread the first couple chapters of this book if you have to. We live in the most affluent country during the most affluent time of history, and yet the average Christian is under a tremendous debt load. It is our sin that put us there, not God! Being financially foolish and expecting God to bless us financially is as crazy as jumping out of an airplane without a parachute and asking God for a miracle as we hurtle toward the ground. Financial problems in churches are the result of us reaping what we have sown. Yes, God will always take care of us, but we have cheated ourselves of blessings because of our stupidity. Our churches struggle because of our own financial sin.

A Biblical Comparison

While everything I have said is Biblical in principle, we might be able to go even farther. An argument can be made that the plan I have laid out is not only Biblical in principle, but is God's specific plan that He intended for us.

> *"In my Father's house are many mansions: if it were not so, I would have told you. I go to prepare a place for you."*
>
> John 14:2

During Bible times, mortgages were not the norm as they are today. In Jewish culture (during Bible times), a young man would not get romantically involved until he was thinking of marriage. During that time, he would live at home and prepare a place for his future wife. Oftentimes this was an addition onto his father's house. When he married his bride, he had no debts, and a place to live. This plan allowed them to survive and thrive during a time of much less affluence when compared to today.

Doesn't this sound like what Christ has done with His church? We are the bride of Christ, are we not? He has gone to prepare a place for us. One day we will be with Him and we won't have a mortgage. It sounds silly to say it that way because we are talking about God, but think how different American Christianity would be if only we followed the same model.

Which teen are you?
Which teen are you raising?

"You Can't Afford Not To"

#13
The Topic Everyone Hates, But Should Love

Many Christians hate the subject of tithing, but every Christian should love it. I almost didn't include this chapter in this book. I didn't want the rest of the advice in this book to be stereotyped away. I didn't want people to roll their eyes or turn their nose up to this book because they thought it was "just another book about tithing." Ultimately, I decided I had to include it because it is just too important.

I would be scared not to tithe.

I have faithfully tithed and given offerings above a tithe since 1990. I have seen God bless me over and over. I have seen God meet needs in my life and meet needs in others through my giving. For those reasons alone I will tithe for the rest of my life. There is another reason, however, and that is that I would be scared not to tithe.

> *"Will a man rob God? Yet ye have robbed me. But ye say, Wherein have we robbed thee? In tithes and offerings."*
>
> Malachi 3:8

"Ye are cursed with a curse: for ye have robbed me, even this whole nation."

Malachi 3:9

"Bring ye all the tithes into the storehouse, that there may be meat in mine house, and prove me now herewith, saith the LORD of hosts, if I will not open you the windows of heaven, and pour you out a blessing, that there shall not be room enough to receive it."

Malachi 3:10

"And I will rebuke the devourer for your sakes, and he shall not destroy the fruits of your ground; neither shall your vine cast her fruit before the time in the field, saith the LORD of hosts."

Malachi 3:11

You have probably have heard those verses many times, but I ask you not to skip them. Please go back to them now and read them slowly and thoughtfully. Think about them a moment before continuing.

God says that they were cursed with a curse because they did not tithe. ***Cursed with a curse!*** Ouch! If there is anyone that I want on my side financially, it is God. I tithe because I love the Lord and because He has told us to, but, truly, I would be afraid not to tithe.

God says that they have robbed from Him. I honestly would rather steal from you, than to steal from God. It would be wiser for me to put my hand into your pocket and grab your wallet than it would be for me to steal from the one who holds my entire life in His hands.

I have seen non-tithers and I have seen their struggles. Meanwhile, I have seen God miraculously provide for tithers. In fact, God will intervene for a tither (to a point) even if they have made other financial mistakes. Tithing trumps your other mistakes. Now, it would be wiser not to make those other mistakes, but tithing is the most important thing you can do financially.

> *"Give, and it shall be given unto you; good measure, pressed down, and shaken together, and running over, shall men give into your bosom. For with the same measure that ye mete withal it shall be measured to you again."*
>
> Luke 6:38

You can't out-give God. As you give, so God will give back to you. Both these passages, by the way, make it plain that you get more than just rewards in heaven for your giving. You get rewards right here, right now on earth. In Malachi, God says He will rebuke the devourer for your sakes if you tithe. In Luke, God says that ***men*** will give into your bosom. Yes, you will have rewards in heaven, but you will also have blessings now.

Don't argue with me that tithing is not for today and that it is part of the law. That's silly. That is another excuse to justify covetousness. It's recorded that Abraham tithed before the law, tithing is recorded in the law, we see tithing in the Old Testament prophets, and Jesus confirmed tithing in the New Testament.

> *"But woe unto you, Pharisees! for ye tithe mint and rue and all manner of herbs, and pass over judgment and the love of God: these ought ye to have done, and not to leave the other undone."*
>
> Luke 11:42

Jesus said not to leave the other undone! He confirmed it in the New Testament. What was the tithe for in the Old Testament? It was for the maintenance of God's work. It provided for the priests, took care of the temple, etc. Likewise the tithe provides for the maintenance of God's work in the New Testament. Bring it into the storehouse, the local church.

Tithing is the most important thing you can do financially.

"The Most Important Chapter"

#14
Why this Material is Needed

Why is this material so needed? Why do we need to follow all of this advice? There are so many reasons. I won't try to list them all. Instead, I want to tell you why I do what I do. I want to tell you why I started implementing these things in my life.

> *"Lay not up for yourselves treasures upon earth, where moth and rust doth corrupt, and where thieves break through and steal:"*
>
> Matthew 6:19

> *"But lay up for yourselves treasures in heaven, where neither moth nor rust doth corrupt, and where thieves do not break through nor steal:"*
>
> Matthew 6:20

> *"For where your treasure is, there will your heart be also."*
>
> Matthew 6:21

My heart. I wanted to love God more. We have looked at Matthew 6:19-21 already in this book. I memorized those verses as a young Christian. I want my heart to be drawn toward the Lord.

I want to be a good steward of everything in my life. I had a high-paying, successful, secular job with a future when I set the course of my life. I was thankful for it and I desperately wanted it to count for God. I think it is a Bible principle that God will expect more from those to whom He gives more. God had given me much, and I believed that He expected much.

> *"His lord said unto him, Well done, good and faithful servant; thou hast been faithful over a few things, I will make thee ruler over many things: enter thou into the joy of thy lord."*
>
> Matthew 25:23

I want to hear that. I want my Lord to say to me well done. That would be worth everything and more. I want God to tell me that I have been faithful over the things He has given me on this earth.

> *"Give, and it shall be given unto you; good measure, pressed down, and shaken together, and running over, shall men give into your bosom. For with the same measure that ye mete withal it shall be measured to you again."*
>
> Luke 6:38

I wanted to be one of the "men" in Luke 6:38. Many people focus on Luke 6:38 and think only of how they will be blessed if they give. I look at it and I notice that God uses "men" to give into your bosom. I not only want to be blessed, I want to be one of those that gets to be used of God to bless others. I want to be one of ***those*** men that God uses to bless others.

"Let him that stole steal no more: but rather let him labour, working with his hands the thing which is good, that he may have to give to him that needeth."
Ephesians 4:28

The whole ***purpose*** for us working is so that we can avoid sin and give to him that needeth. This book is not about getting rich! It is about having more money so that you can be used of the Lord more. That is important to have straight in your mind.

Success is dangerous.

If you approach this book for the wrong reasons - to get rich so you can spend more on yourself - then this book really won't help you.

"But they that will be rich fall into temptation and a snare, and into many foolish and hurtful lusts, which drown men in destruction and perdition."
I Timothy 6:9

Some people serve the Lord when they are struggling and turn away from Him when things go well. That is why they say success is dangerous. That is why it is important to know ***why*** you want to do better financially.

I want to live this book so I can do cool things for the Lord with the money He gives me. I think about Russell Anderson and the hundreds of churches he has started, the number of colleges he has helped, and the number of people he is indirectly responsible for bringing to Christ (through the works and soul winners he supports- it's millions, by the way). That is awesome! I want to do that. I might not be able to do it on his scale, but I want to do as much of it as I can.

I want you to be blessed, and if you follow the ideas and advice in this book, you will be (sowing and reaping works)! I want you to be happy and I don't want you to suffer needlessly because of financial mistakes. You ***will*** be blessed, too. Russell Anderson has not only given much to the Lord, he also gets to drive a Jaguar. :-) Not that I am saying you will be rich like him, but rather that following these principles will better your financial situation. I want families reared in these principles to enjoy all of the blessings that God would desire to give them, for them not to reap any bitter financial fruit, and to be in the perfect will of God.

More than wanting to see you blessed, though, I want to see God's work blessed. I want to see an army of people giving to the Lord's work in the same way that Russell Anderson does. As God blesses you, you will have the means to help God's work. As you start this process, nail your motives down. Write them down. This, or something like it, would be a good thing for you to write in your prayer journal:

> "God, as I start trying to improve my finances, I ask you to forgive all of my stupid financial mistakes of the past. I'm asking you to bless me so that I can bless others. Help me to grow so that you can trust me with your finances and help me be a good steward of them. If you bless me financially, I promise to use it for you."

I believe you will be blessed more if your motives are right, if you intend to use your gain for the Lord. Oh, you will still get to enjoy those blessings as the money flows through you, but it is important that you let God know that your motives are not about yourself.

What are your motives?

"Postscript"

#15
The After Action Report

"So, Pastor Krohn, how has this worked out for you and your family?" Pretty well, thank you for asking. My son has saved lots of money. It's not quite as much as he had hoped, but that is mostly due to his ministry decisions - he purposely turned down a higher paying job because it would have interfered (time-wise) with his ability to serve the Lord. My oldest daughter has a good job as a phlebotomist in the out-patient lab of a major hospital. Both live at home and are continuing to save. My youngest is on track for college and nursing. All is well, financially. More importantly, they all seem to love the Lord. Praise Jesus! (keep praying)

However, there is a new thought/idea that I feel like I should share. I am continuing to learn and grow and this is something that has become more prominent in my thinking the last 4-5 years. Everything up until now in this book, I have been dogmatic about. I have lived it and can vouch for it first hand. What I am about to share with you, I am less dogmatic about. I ***think*** I am learning this, but I have not lived it yet. So, take the following with a grain of salt.

My oldest is just about to graduate from our Bible Institute, he has saved up money, and the next phase of his life is looming in front of him. So, he should use that saved up money to buy a house, right? Maybe.

THE PARADIGM SHIFT

There has been a paradigm shift in jobs in America. Once upon a time, you got a good paying job, worked there for 30-35 years, and retired from the company. That changed in America in the 70s and 80s. The engineering job market that I entered out of college was not that way. With downsizing, it was becoming increasingly more common to have to move companies once or twice during your career. The good jobs were still there, you just couldn't count on them forever.

Well, the shift has continued. Good paying jobs are just not as plentiful as they once were. In our area in New York, we have families losing their jobs or being moved out of state all of the time. The paradigm has shifted from *"Good paying job for life"* to *"Good paying job, but may have to switch companies"* to *"Hard to find a good paying job."*

This has brought me to the position that entrepreneurship and owning a business may just be the direction some Christians should head in. When you do that, in effect, you are creating your own job, one that usually pays much more than what is currently available on the market today. It is also one that doesn't get downsized or moved out of state. That money that my son has saved - maybe it should go into a house, but maybe it should go into a business.

I know that you can lose money in a business. Plus, I know you have to be the right kind of person. You have to be driven, a hard worker, detail oriented, etc. to own your business. I hesitated to bring this up because I haven't lived this yet. However, I have seen others do very well with it and I would feel guilty if I didn't bring it up because of the paradigm shift in the job market.

There are stable businesses out there. Perhaps a franchise of a chain with a proven business model. Something that has an ROI (return on investment) of 2-3 years. We are looking at some options that would effectively double to triple my son's yearly income and require less hours at work (it would enable even more ministry). He might own the business for the next 50 years. That is a huge life impact. Of course, we couldn't even be thinking about this if he hadn't been saving his cash because he wouldn't be in the position to buy a business at his age.

For the right person, owning your own business might just be the will of God. It is something that all Christians should pray about.

Owning your own business might be the will of God for some Christians.

APPENDIX

APPENDIX

Notes, Resources, and Some Odds and Ends

CHAPTER 6 NOTE - COUPLING

In chapter six I mentioned that you will likely spend more if you use a credit card. This is due to "decoupling." "Coupling" refers to the degree to which your purchase and your payment are bound together psychologically. Credit cards decouple - they separate the purchase from the payment.

Credit cards do this in a number of ways.

$ They increase the time period between purchase and payment.

$ They combine many purchases into one payment. Because of this, when you pay your credit card bill, you don't associate it with any particular purchase.

$ The fact that we often use a credit card for many types of purchases makes that disassociation even more pronounced.

$ Credit cards also decrease coupling because they have a lower vividness. Handing over cash is much more vivid. Credit cards merely require signing a slip of paper, and now sometimes we don't even have to do that.

CHAPTER 6 NOTE - CUTTING UP CREDIT CARDS

In chapter six I told you to cut up your credit cards. This can be an emotional experience for some people. I've heard it described to me like it was taking the training wheels off of your bike for the first time. You knew you could do it, but for the first couple tries you were afraid of falling. Credit cards create peace of mind for many people and cutting up their security blanket is a VERY hard thing to do. For the Christian, this should be easy, but often it is not.

I have also heard that people can grow emotionally attached to their first credit card. I suspect this to be true. There must be a reason why companies market cards so heavily to college students. That also might be because of the financial ignorance that is rampant in that population.

CHAPTER 7 NOTE - MORTGAGE INTEREST TAX DEDUCTION

In chapter seven I mentioned that your mortgage interest ***may*** result in a tax deduction. It will not always result in a full deduction because it depends on your tax situation. Not everyone itemizes on their taxes (although most Christians should because of charitable giving). If you are not itemizing now, then it is unlikely that mortgage interest will get you the full amount. If itemizing wasn't quite worth your while, perhaps the mortgage interest puts you over the top, but perhaps the first few thousand of your itemizing gets you past your standard deduction and the last few thousand of your interest gets you some benefit.

The $1000 savings on the $7000 in interest is based on being in the 15% tax bracket. The savings could be higher if you are in the 28% bracket, but none of this changes the main thrust of my point. While the mortgage interest you pay may get you a percentage back because of a tax deduction, that is not as good as keeping 100% of your money!

Interest Rate Calculator

A great resource to have is an interest rate/ mortgage calculator. Go to my church's website:

www.myground.org

and look for "Resources." In that area you will find an Excel spreadsheet that you can download. You can input all of the variables of your loan - the interest rate, the term, the number of payments made, etc. It will tell you how much interest is in each payment, how much interest you have paid so far, how much interest you will pay by the end of the loan, etc. It is just a very useful tool. As we find other tools, we will post them there.

How to Get Out of Debt

I focused mainly on principles and practical advice in this book. While I touched on how to get out of debt in the chapter on credit cards, I did not go into detail. If you are in debt, you should follow the advice in that section - cut up your credit cards, get your high interest rate credit card balances transferred onto a low introductory rate card, spend less, etc.

In addition, most sources that I have read strongly recommend paying off your smallest loan first. The idea is that you want to create a snowball effect. Say you have a credit card with a minimum payment of $50 per month and it is your smallest loan. If you have $100 each month of disposable income, you put all $100 on that small loan so that you are paying $150 per month. When that is paid off, you now have increased your available income each month from $100 to $150. You then take all of that $150 and put it on your next smallest loan. As you pay off loans, you increase your free cash and then you take all of that free cash and apply it to the next loan. This creates a snowball whereby you pay off loans faster and faster. It also allows you to see some progress.

Cash Reserve

Again, most sources that I read strongly recommend a cash reserve. Some suggest a reserve as high as six months of living expenses. That may be extreme and it may not be realistic in everyone's case, but the idea of a cash reserve is important. You will have big bills: the furnace will quit on you in the middle of winter, and the car will break down. If you are not going to run to the credit card, you have to have a cash reserve (and the Lord, of course).

Budgeting

Budgeting deserves its own book. If you make a realistic budget and discipline yourself to live by that budget, you will spend less and have a better financial situation than you would otherwise.

NOT EXHAUSTIVE

Obviously this book does not cover all there is on finances. That was not my goal. Instead, I wanted to hit the critical things in a book that was highly accessible. If I tried to put everything in this book, frankly, I would just drive up the cost of the book and intimidate people. This book is meant to grab all of the "low-hanging fruit". If Christians just did these simple things, it would be revolutionary. Once you have exhausted this book, I would encourage you to delve into other resources and continue your study on finances.

Of course, this book also contains many controversial things that you will not find elsewhere. It also puts these things in a spiritual light. It is not only practical, but spiritual - but it is not an exhaustive book on finances.

COMMON SENSE

The old saying is, "common sense is not so common." That is so true. My very practical look at money will undoubtedly offend people, but Jesus was very practical. I dealt with this in the book already, but I want to give you an example of Jesus' practicality.

> *"After these things Jesus walked in Galilee: for he would not walk in Jewry, because the Jews sought to kill him."*
>
> John 7:1

This verse shows Jesus' common sense and practical side. Jesus knew that the Jews wanted to kill Him so He avoided them. Jesus was God and we know that He had nothing to fear from those Jews. Jesus was not going to die before His time (*"my time is not yet come"*). So, why does He care that the Jews wanted to kill Him? Why does He avoid walking in Jewry?

> *"For even hereunto were ye called: because Christ also suffered for us, leaving us an example, that ye should follow his steps:"*
>
> I Peter 2:21

> *"For I have given you an example, that ye should do as I have done to you."*
>
> John 13:15

Jesus did things as an example for us! Of course! Even though He had nothing to fear from those Jews that were trying to kill Him, He wants us to see in His life that we are supposed to use common sense.

Yes, there will be times where God will lead us against common sense, but those are special occasions. There were times where Christ was led right into the middle of an angry mob that was trying to kill him and He was miraculously saved, but those are the exceptions. They did not happen every day.

We should be willing to follow God wherever He leads us, but barring special leading, we should not ignore obvious, common sense, practical things. This includes your finances!

LIFE INSURANCE

There is a difference between "whole" and "term" life insurance. Term insurance only pays out a death benefit. Whole life pays out a death benefit, but will also give you a small monthly return after you get to a certain age. While I think it is wise to have some term insurance to help provide for your family in the event of your death, I am not a fan of whole life.

While the concept of whole life sounds good, it is much more expensive. In reality, what they are doing is collecting more money from you, investing your money, making money on your money, and giving you some back as you get older. So much could go wrong along the way. If you let your policy lapse, you lose your benefit. If you have a short term emergency, you don't have access to your money. Plus, at the end, you get back less money than if you had invested it yourself. How is this a good deal? Buy an inexpensive term policy and put the rest of your extra cash down on your debt.

What is especially disturbing to me is that I have heard reports of financial counselors who sell whole life policies. Why? To make money. Imagine a financial counselor sitting down with you and helping you with your budget. You are looking for help and an "expert" is willing to help you. At the end of the budget, there is some disposable cash available in your budget and it just happens to be enough to buy this whole life policy that the counselor tells you that you need. Talk about a conflict of interest! Any financial counselor who does this is not helping you, they are helping themselves.

If a financial counselor sees that you have debt and still recommends you buy the whole life policy? That financial counselor is either incompetent or a completely self-interested individual who is taking advantage of the trust that people put into him. It would be more honest if they called themselves a life insurance salesman instead of a financial counselor.

GOVERNMENT AND OTHER AID

If this book hasn't gotten me in trouble already, this last bit might do it. There are those that strongly oppose believers accepting any kind of government assistance - as if it is an unspiritual thing to do. I just don't understand it. Besides being unpractical, it doesn't make logical sense to me. Where does the government get its money? Taxpayers - including many, many believers. The government takes this money from us and I do not always agree with what they do with it. I wish they would not take this money and that government was smaller and less intrusive on our lives. However, as long as the government is taking money away from believers, then I am all for some of that money going back to believers. Here are some things to think about.

The Earned Income Credit - Most already know about this tremendous tax credit. However, I mention it only to make a point. When you accept this tax credit, you are accepting government aid. If you accept this, then why not other aid?

H.E.A.P - I don't know if this is available in every state, but this stands for the Home Energy Assistance Program. In New York, if you are accepted for this aid, money will be sent directly to your fuel provider to help pay for your heating bills.

Food Pantry - These are not necessarily run by the government. Often they are run by private institutions. A typical eligibility guideline is 180% of the government-declared poverty level. This means that a family of five can have access to them on a weekly basis even if they make close to $50,000 per year (in 2011).

Free Medical Care - Many states have free medical insurance for low-income families. This has nothing to do with any federal program (that I know of). New York had this long before health care reform was discussed.

Charity Care - Many hospitals have programs whereby you can apply for coverage of your medical bills. If money is tight for you, it does not hurt to ask.

Food Stamps, Wick, etc. - There are many federal and state programs that provide food and/or milk for low-income families.

You might not qualify or even be interested in the above programs. However, if times are bad for you financially, it is well worth your time to spend an hour on the Internet looking. It is well worth your time to call your local town hall and ask about available assistance. Believers paid into those programs through their taxes and believers should be able to get some of that money back.

$100 WITH A GREAT STORY

After hearing my Sunday School lesson on finances, Dr. Russell Anderson raved about it and told my church that he would ask God to whip me if I didn't write a book on it. Over lunch, he took out this $100 bill and slid it across the table to me. He told me that he was buying the first book and that I had to write the book now because money had changed hands. ***He obviously thinks what I have to say about finances is important*** and he is richer (and probably more generous) than you or I will ever be.

Please don't ignore this book!

SCRIPTURE INDEX

OTHER BOOKS FROM GROUND & PILLAR

BIBLICAL YOUTH WORK: A very Biblical look at youth ministry written by someone in the trenches for twenty plus years. It breaks a lot of conventions and deals with some of the problems in youth ministries today. This book not only looks at how to run an activity, but lays out the Biblical basis and purpose of youth work, deals with important topics, and examines relationships. Not just a book for youth leaders - ***this book is for teens, parents, and pastors alike!***

VOYAGE: A ten lesson discipleship book that is great for new converts. It is inexpensive and unintimidating to someone who is cautious about committing to a long discipleship program. It starts with an apologetic for the Christian faith and the Bible and gives new believers a good start for their growth. Good for classes as well as in home Bible study.

NEW TESTAMENT COMPANION: This is designed to be used for your daily devotions in the New Testament. Unlike other devotional books, the focus in this one is the daily Bible reading. Each page of the book has background information for the day's reading, in formation on the historical setting, and has some simple questions to answer. It gives structure to your devotion time.